Have a nice weekend
I think you're interesting

Lucy Holt

the poetry business

Published 2021 by
New Poets List
The Poetry Business
Campo House,
54 Campo Lane,
Sheffield S1 2EG

Copyright © Lucy Holt 2021
All Rights Reserved

ISBN 978-1-912196-60-9
eBook ISBN 978-1-912196-61-6
Typeset by The Poetry Business
Printed by Biddles, Sheffield

Smith|Doorstop Books are a member of Inpress:
www.inpressbooks.co.uk

Distributed by NBN International, 1 Deltic Avenue,
Rooksley, Milton Keynes MK13 8LD

The Poetry Business gratefully acknowledges
the support of Arts Council England.

Contents

5	Blue light, morning
6	Entertaining
8	My entire life
9	What good is a muesli woman
10	Clive who walks across the sands
11	COS woman
12	Folding patterns
13	Lessons in gifting
14	Birds as consolation
15	The death of the living room
17	A dedication or a type of portal in fact
18	There is no word for this in German
19	Ghosts I
20	Ghosts II
21	Ghosts III
22	Women I know but in real life
23	Winter hands
24	Timperley
25	Have a nice weekend I think you're interesting

Blue light, morning

In the backlit mirror
of nighttime

a performance
we assemble at its perimeter

cheeks swollen with
ripeness as a language

it's not news that red lipstick
has always looked good

that eyelash curlers
are terrifying to men

yet I devour intimacy
full ponds of description

twelve and a half thousand words
for *sort of* coral

relearning backwards
gestures of youth

knowing things named for revenge
rarely bring it

Entertaining

Stood by the patio doors you tell me what
voice like cut glass means
and I want to go inside

concertinaed open
like those doors
by your once-hospitable arms

I'm doing my joke
about how I only date the sons of mothers
who have appeared on Woman's Hour

how my own mother calls this war
I am calling this confirmation bias
I am calling it a line in the sand

but you do look exquisite
when you do quizzes
when you know absolutely nothing at all

so I flirt for practice
with your mother's boss who is American
and here for some reason

on the drive home
I push my palms to the sunroof
feeling for weak points

as we take the lanes around the airport
I say *I thought you meant*
like a brightness or verve

I close my eyes
and pretend I'm driving
all I've ever known is how to win

My entire life

In another life I'd have been an
events coordinator
or maybe mothered foals

when the doctor feels his way
around the back of my neck I could
be anyone who has ever lived

I talk to everyone spectacularly
even the burglar
even the baby

at the ice rink the instructor
tells me to stop thinking
before I jump

but how
I'm just anecdotes and
all the different flats I've lived in

What good is a muesli woman

or a woman made of gorse?
One day you'll wake up and realise
I was right about everything
there is no such thing as girlfriend material
I only made you up
in Go Outdoors

Clive who walks across the sands

I sunk model ships in the sands
before they were the sands
you don't understand death at sea
when you're five

there is no glamour
in the unmetaphor of edgelands
but there is Clive
who walks across the sands and he knows

I've never sulked coldly
on the sea wall pebble dashed
had chips with goth friends
that sort of thing

my cobwebs are mine I love them
but this place never was
I wouldn't know a single pub
to take you to

how dare we think of swimming
we don't know
the right words for
tragedy, memory

it just lashes it down
we talk of safe passage
and of home but there's
only Clive and his sticks and mud

COS woman

I have drawn my edges
in an idea of resistance

a windsock woman
I am capacious and shakeable

I curate balloons in black
a seaside cut-out

serious like wearing lead clogs
to breakfast

I know small objects
can be talismans!

there exists
a parsable language of things!

in charity shops I wonder
what will become

of my short torso
my indelicate waist

the hot protrusions of my knees
under desks in summer

Folding patterns

What sun is this nightdress?
grey-white like the bedding you buy
when you move back
I understand the meaning of stripes
in some medical contexts
but I've never known what to do
with my hands

when sitting up my stomach
is an oil slick of lip gloss
there are six bulldozers
lined up outside but still
they leave the quizzes on
with the sound turned down

it's not so hard to follow
if you know what you're looking for
twice I've been so angry I could eat myself
twice I've done exactly that

Lessons in gifting

What does it mean to be a woman today
reading the slogan *lingerie for women who don't do lingerie*
    wondering to what extent you do?

I have owned the same pyjama bottoms for a decade
there never was a shirt
    I don't remember how you look when you sleep

I know theories of spontaneity and kindness
but you have to be a flowers person for people to buy you flowers
    for once I am not talking about men

on the radio they want to hear about your local high street
I didn't know anything about yellow roses and
    I am gently furious there is so much to learn

Birds as consolation

I'm jealous of stupid birds who are sincere
and can murmurate – yes – murmurate
without knowing
how embarrassing it is to lean in

It's called murmuration I say
which isn't the point
the point is I'm drowning
the point is that I've never drunk-cried
outside a nightclub before
never said I love you this
close to a dual carriageway

my hands are so very far away
and I believe it is possible to see through time

how gorgeous they are
the stupid birds in their big empty sky
how perfect it must be

The death of the living room

The carpet is worn down
from looping back

in the kitchen there's shouting
it is female

after lunchtime wine
disbelief more readily suspends itself

in the folds:
leopard print on leopard print

hospitality as hospitality
the implied TV on TV

propped on sofa arm I have gladly forgotten
what I've been asked to forget

about bodies of water
their long memories

the reverse side
of the known universe

how things accumulate over time
or don't

I too have sheltered
from the rain

in the company of men
who look tall under railway arches

with their hard u's and
inscrutable business practices

have misjudged
the passage of time

more than once
I have assembled a ritual of stools

left the hollow door ajar
raised my eye line to a false horizon

and winced like a bird
in the half-second before flight

A dedication or a type of portal in fact

I want to dedicate everything I've ever written
to the mothers-in-law I will never have
to Hildegard and the bees
but I know that wouldn't be fair:
this is a wormhole

I'm planning a poem about precipices
and three separate essays
on listening to your gut

while feeling through the dark
for the exit
at least I have learned
how to secrete myself
in rockpools
some of the fundamentals
of urban planning

at times I have known
what it feels like
to make you laugh

over dinner
in rockpools,
goodbye

There is no word for this in German

In the third decade of the twenty-first century
picking lint off a jumper is no longer a radical act of kindness
your friends are all married or dead

In the third decade of the twenty-first century
it is illegal to be bored
of your most persistent self

In the third decade of the twenty-first century
you have stopped shopping for clothes
there is a group chat for all mankind you are admin

In the third decade of the twenty-first century
it really is all about finding a workout
that works for you

In the third decade of the twenty-first century
all your exes turn thirty-one
you bookmark an article on Saturn's return

In the third decade of the twenty-first century
an old woman is brought down from the attic
all covered in mulch

In the third decade of the twenty-first century
you begin to experiment with non-ironic rage
there's a word for this you are unstoppable

Ghosts I

It was women at looms
who invented computing
the threads, they're ours

ones and zeros like cheek textures
unsentimental holes
punched into cards

the email thread isn't a real thing
dining al desko isn't a real thing

our tongues
our most laborious selves
unreal in empty factories
shipping containers
filled with the stuffness of stuff
girl ghosts
shared hands kissing like
two cursors blinking
and so very present
in the same Google doc

Ghosts II

Empathy is a creature
made of historic buildings
which are different to romance
or are containers for it

empathy is leaving before you're asked to
(in pubs, in love)

empathy is remembering that
whilst it is possible to bridge a gap
romantically speaking
between Milton Keynes and London
there's so little point
in saying so

Ghosts III

2013 was a good one
I spun yarns of my cleverest self
was brilliantly desired from places
as far flung as Carlisle by men who
loved cricket and felt things strongly
a dangerous sport

It's unwise to speak ill of
all those ghosts
in threads half-lived
(what if it was just a hunch?)
better to imagine things
were different then
and love yourself
and all those splendid tricks

Women I know but in real life

The morning Sally from *Coronation Street*
was in my yoga class
I could barely contain myself
in half-pigeon
thinking about what it must be like
to have a consistent sense of self

when I think of Sally from Coronation Street
I think of hot tubs and conservatories
of the long journey from the front door

I think in half-pigeon
about waterways and interruptions
of my twelve future husbands
their complete forgiveness
and how they will die

and inevitably
of the patio
and corpse pose
and how from one week to the next
we forget, we forget, we forget

Winter hands

The shops were heaving
and you asked whether it was a SAD lamp
I needed instead
knowing it was neither eye creams
nor timescales of understanding
nor an abundance of choice

I was better at jokes anyway
you would not stop calling me remarkable
you simply would not stop

I don't believe in premonitions
just that days fill from the bottom up
like sand at the shallow end of the pool
so we called it
as if we always knew of quicksand

Timperley

Leisure centres
the stench of them like cabbage pie in Moscow

I have loved men from the coast who cannot swim
I am always seeking a challenge

you've knocked me sideways:
there are hometowns and then there's this

when they talk of the palimpsest of place
I don't think they mean Timperley

Have a nice weekend I think you're interesting

My favourite topic is our mutual friends
of which we have none

I have never been this funny
you are nice to people in shops

in the gallery there is
hot pink tape on our shoes

I feel like a god
an art gallery god

I am face blind apart from
you sometimes

and at night you roll me
across the wet grass

to a gentle stop
outside my mother's porch